The U.S.
Marine Corps
in World War II

Steve Crawford holds a postgraduate degree in military history from the University of York, Great Britain. After graduating, he worked for the British Defence Intelligence Staff, undertaking numerous secret foreign assignments. After leaving British intelligence, he became a freelance military historian. He currently lives in the south of England.

Also by Steve Crawford

Deadly Fighting Skills of the World
Military Hardware of World War II
SAS Gulf Warriors: The Story Behind Bravo Two Zero
Tanks of World War II
The SAS at Close Quarters: Great Battles of the SAS
SAS Encyclopedia: The Definitive Companion to the World's Crack Regiment
Twenty-First Century Military Helicopters
Twenty-First Century Small Arms: The World's Great Infantry Weapons
Twenty-First Century Submarines: Undersea Vessels of Today's Navies
Twenty-First Century Warships
The Eastern Front Day by Day, 1941–45

The U.S. Marine Corps
in World War II

THE STORIES BEHIND THE PHOTOS

Steve Crawford

POTOMAC BOOKS, INC.
WASHINGTON, D.C.

Potomac Books, Inc.
22841 Quicksilver Drive
Dulles, Virginia 20166

Copyright © 2007 The Brown Reference Group plc

Library of Congress Cataloging-in-Publication Data

Crawford, Steve, 1960–
The U.S. Marine Corps in World War II: the stories behind the photos/.
Steve Crawford. -- 1st ed.
    p. cm.
  Includes index.
ISBN: 978-1-59797-131-7 (alk. paper)
1. United States. Marine Corps--History--World War 1939-1945. 2. United
States. Marine Corps--History--World War 1939-1945--Pictorial works. 3.
World War, 1939-1945--Campaigns. 4. World War,
1939-1945--Campaigns--Pictorial works. 5. World War,
1939-1945--Photography. 6. War photography--United States. I. Title. II.
Title: United States Marine Corps in World War Two.
  D769.369.C73 2007
  940.54'5973--dc22

                              2007012016

Printed in The People's Republic of China

First Edition

10 9 8 7 6 5 4 3 2 1

Editorial and Design
The Brown Reference Group plc
8 Chapel Place
Rivington Street
London
EC2A 3DQ
www.brownreference.com

Senior Editor: Peter Darman
Technical Editor: Keith Wardell
Proofreader: Alan Marshall
Designer: Lynne Ross
Production Director: Alastair Gourlay
Index: Indexing Specialists (UK) Ltd

Picture credits
All images from The Robert Hunt Library except the following:
Al Perry: 78–79.
Corbis: 126–127

Front cover and spine: U.S. Marines on Betio Island, November 1943.

Back cover: Clearing caves of Japanese defenders on Okinawa, June 1945.

Pages 2–3: Marines on Roi Island watch as a Japanese bunker blows up on nearby Namur Island, February 1944.

Contents

1942   6

1943   34

1944   76

1945   100

Index   128

Leatherneck machine gunners

Troops of the 3rd Battalion, 4th Marine Regiment, marching on Bataan in March 1942 ❶. They are pulling .3in M1917 machine guns protected by covers and mounted on tripods ❷. Each machine gun weighed 18.6kg (41lb) and the tripod 24.1kg (53.1lb). An effective weapon, it was initially used to equip Marine battalion weapons companies. The uniforms on display are indicative of early war Marine wear. Though the M1 steel helmet was adopted before the war, the Marines fought their first battles in M1917A1 "dishpan" helmets ❸. Made of manganese steel, they were usually painted forest green. The cotton khaki summer service uniform ❹ was impractical for field use and was replaced by so-called "utilities". On their feet the men are wearing ankle-high field service boots ("Boondockers") ❺. When the Americans surrendered on Corregidor on 6 May 1942, the 4th Marines burned their colours and went into captivity.

Prelude to the Bataan Death March

Japanese soldiers ❶ stand guard over US Marines ❷ following the surrender of Corregidor in May 1942, some of the 11,000 Americans and Filipinos who fell into Japanese hands. This photograph was taken before the infamous "Death March" and the cruel imprisonment that followed. During the march from Bataan to Camp O'Donnell north of Manila the guards deprived the prisoners of food and water, and murdered any stragglers. According to the Bushido code, soldiers who surrendered rather than fight to the death dishonoured themselves and forfeited any right to humane treatment. To make matters worse, the captives had previously subsisted for months on partial rations, which meant many started out in a weakened state. The guard nearest the camera is wearing a field cap with a neck guard ❸ and has a bayonet ❹ attached to his Arisaka bolt-action rifle ❺, which had a magazine capacity of five rounds.

Striking back against Tokyo's outposts

Marines storm ashore on Beach Red ❶, Guadalcanal, the Solomons, on 7 August 1942. The first wave consisted of the reinforced 5th Marines (minus the 2d Battalion). There were no Japanese troops or guns on the beach. The first Marines waded ashore at 09:10 hours on a 1463m (4800ft) front, with the reinforced 1st Battalion on the right and the reinforced 3rd Battalion on the left. The vessels are Landing Craft, Personnel, Large ❷, each capable of carrying up to 36 troops. These had a solid block of pine at the bow ❸ to allow them to run at full speed over floating obstacles, sandbars and right up on to the beach. Of interest is that the M1 helmet has replaced the "dishpan" helmet. The Marine in the centre appears to have an M1936 canvas field bag on his back (its shoulder strap could be configured into double straps to allow it to be carried as a backpack) ❹ plus an M1941 haversack at his waist ❺.

Interrupting the enemy's midday meal

Marines sweep through a recently deserted Japanese camp ❶ on Guadalcanal in early September 1942 (note the food still on the table ❷). The trees show no signs of combat – they have not been hit by bullets and artillery rounds. Though the M1 helmet ❸ is now standard issue, canvas leggings and Boondockers remain common footwear ❹. Armament still consists of Springfield rifles ❺, though on Guadalcanal the M1 Garand semi-automatic rifle was introduced to Marine Corps service. It was phased into service one regiment at a time. These men ❻ are from the 1st Marine Division, "The Old Breed", activated on 1 February 1941. Landing on Guadalcanal on 7 August 1942, the 1st Marine Division fought on the island until December, when it was withdrawn to Australia for a rest and refit. Commanded by Major-General Alexander A. Vandegrift, it comprised the 1st, 5th, 7th, 11th (artillery) and 17th (engineer) Marines.

USMC heavy metal on Guadalcanal

An M2A4 light tank ❶ of the corps on Guadalcanal, 5 September 1942. Only the A Companies of the 1st and 2d Tank Battalions operated these vehicles, and this tank is from A Company, 1st Tank Battalion. When they landed on the island the tanks encountered virtually no resistance. They therefore accompanied the infantry across the Tenaru River to establish a defensive perimeter around the airfield called Henderson Field. They went on to perform airfield security duty and took part in counterattacks. The M2A4's crew comprised a commander/gunner ❷ in the left of the turret, a loader in the right rear of the turret, a driver in the left front of the hull, and an assistant driver in the right front of the hull. The main gun was a 37mm M5 ❸, with a shrouded recoil cylinder underneath ❹. Note the .3in M1919A4 machine gun in the anti-aircraft role behind the commander ❺ and the same weapon in the sponson ❻.

Outdated artillery support on Guadalcanal

A battery of Marine 155mm howitzers belonging to the 4th Battalion, 11th Marines ❶, on Guadalcanal, 12 September 1942. These guns are M1918 models ❷, a French design which was modified by the Americans. The latter added steel disc wheels ❸, heavy pneumatic tyres ❹ and air brakes in an effort to adapt the gun for high-speed travel. Served by a crew of 14 ❺, the gun had a limited traverse and insufficient range: 11.5km (7.1 miles). Guadalcanal was the only combat use of the M1918, it being replaced by the 155mm M1A1 medium gun. Marine regiment nomenclature during the war is interesting. The 1st to 9th Marines and 21st to 29th Marines were infantry regiments; 10th–15th Marines were artillery; and 16th–20th Marines were engineers. The word "Regiment" was not included in their designation, unlike divisions, which were always given their full title, i.e. 1st Marine Division as opposed to the regiment: 1st Marines.

Grabbing a rest before fighting the Japanese

A relaxed group of Marines on Guadalcanal in late 1942. This picture presents an interesting display of Marine uniform items. Though armament still comprises M1903 Springfield bolt-action rifles ❶ and M1905 bayonets ❷, and even World War I-type grenade vests ❸, uniforms have at least been updated. The men are wearing two-piece uniforms made of herringbone twill (HBT), referred to as "utilities" and "dungarees". First issued on 10 November 1941, they comprised a shirt with three flapless pockets and trousers with front and hip pockets. The shirt had USMC stencilled above a "globe and anchor" on the left breast pocket. The webbing was commonly referred to as "782 gear" after the form on which a Marine signed for his clothing and equipment. Note the entrenching tool ❹, ammunition pouches ❺ and canteen ❻. Marine webbing was usually tan coloured, with most items being marked USMC on the back or under a flap.

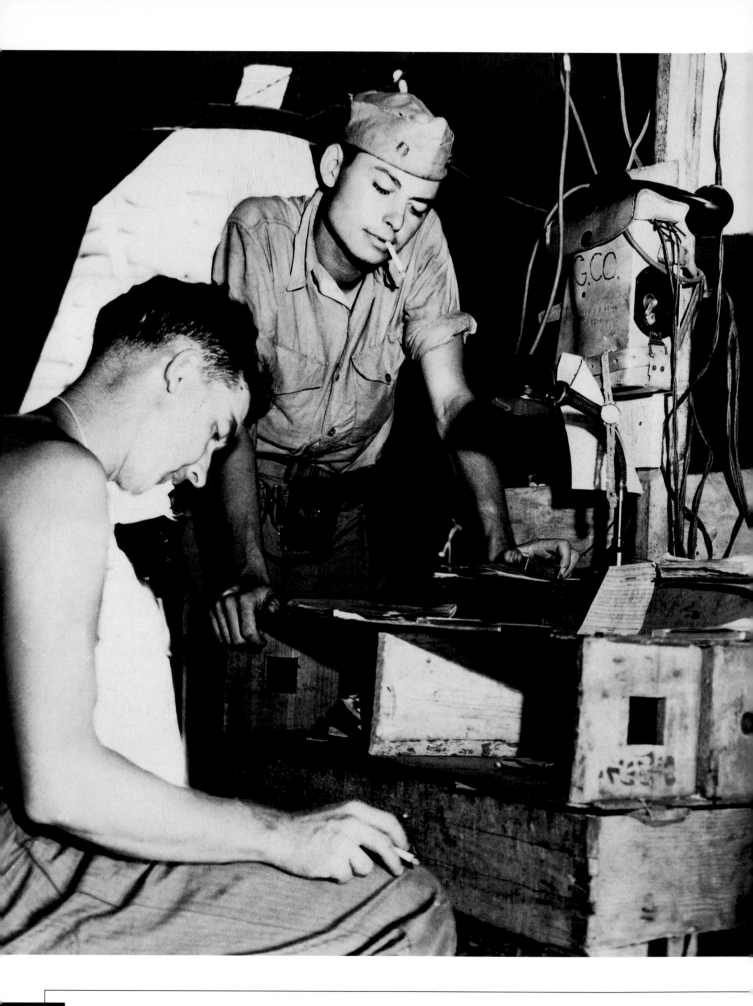

US Marine message centre on Guadalcanal

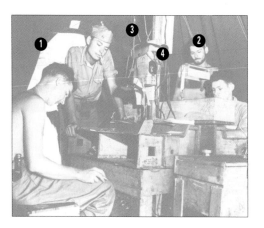

Good communications are integral to success in war. On Guadalcanal one of the first technical tasks performed by the Marines after they had landed was to establish an effective communications system between commanders and frontline units. This is one of the message centres set up on the island ❶, where calls from outposts were received ❷ and passed on to head-quarters, and vice-versa (the Marines strung telephone lines ❸ in the jungle and they converged at centres such as this one). The Corps used field telephones ❹ widely, both the Marine MCT-1 model and the Army's EE-8. Interestingly, the first Navajo code talkers were employed on Guadalcanal. They would verbally transmit messages in Navajo to a receiving code talker writing them down in English on a message pad. Unfortunately, on Guadalcanal commanders failed to grasp the concept and used the code talkers as regular radio operators or messengers.

The misery of a Pacific island campaign

Four Marines ❶ wade through water to their tents ❷ on Guadalcanal, in a camp ❸ near Henderson Field (named after Major Lofton Henderson, the first Marine pilot killed in action, at the Battle of Midway). Rainfall is extremely heavy on the island, and this, together with an average temperature in the high 80s, results in an unhealthy climate in which to live, or fight. Disease was striking down men in numbers equal to battle casualties. Afflictions included gastroenteritis, which weakened those who suffered its crippling stomach cramps. In addition, there were tropical fungus infections, collectively known as "jungle rot", which produced uncomfortable rashes on men's feet, armpits, elbows and crotches, a product of always being wet (either from rain or sweat). Also, Marines' damp clothing ❹ and bedding ❺ contributed to the toll of skin and fungal infections. Finally, there were also hundreds of cases of malaria.

Marine Corps commanders on Guadalcanal

Three top-ranking Marine officers discuss tactics on Guadalcanal. They are, from left to right: Major-General A. Vandegrift ❶, Colonel Gerald Thomas ❷ and Colonel Merritt Edson ❸. Vandegrift, commander of the 1st Marine Division, was awarded the Navy Cross for the attack on Guadalcanal, Tulagi and Gavutu in the Solomon Islands on 7 August 1942, and the Medal of Honor for the subsequent campaign between August and December. Thomas was appointed Chief of Staff of the division in September 1942. Merritt "Red Mike" Edson led the 1st Marine Raider Battalion, which defeated a Japanese attempt to retake Henderson Field on 12 September, called the Battle of Edson's Ridge. Note the khaki cotton shirts ❹ with patch breast pockets ❺ secured by buttoned flaps. When khaki shirts were worn in the field, tan neckties were discarded. Web belts and pistol holsters are also on display ❻.

Browning heavy machine gun on the perimeter

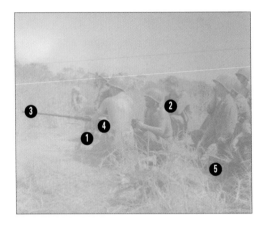

A Marine Corps Browning HBM2 .5in machine gun ❶ fires at Japanese positions west of the Matanikua River on Guadalcanal, November 1942. By this time the Japanese on the island were on the defensive, having lost 3500 dead during an abortive attack against Marine positions on 23–24 October. The HBM2 (HB means heavy barrel) in Corps service was often used as an anti-aircraft weapon, though the absence of Japanese aircraft over Guadalcanal made this role redundant. M2 machine guns were not assigned dedicated crews and were thus often manned by scratch crews ❷ when used on the frontline. The gun had a heavy barrel ❸ to absorb heat during sustained fire. When first produced in 1933 it had a barrel length of 914mm (36in), increased to 1143mm (45in) after 1938. The gun weighed 38kg (84lb); the M3 tripod 19.9kg (44lb). The weapon was fed by a 110-round metal link belt ❹, carried in ammunition boxes ❺.

A Marine Corps marches on its stomach

Marines ❶ line up to be served a meal on Guadalcanal. On the frontline the men ate C and K rations. C rations consisted of prepared meals, such as meat and beans and stew, and biscuits, candy and a concentrated beverage powder for breakfast, all packed in tin cans. K rations included a small can of cheese or meat paste, biscuits, candy, beverage powder, chewing gum and two cigarettes. Eaten cold, K rations were adequate but unappetising. Men did not carry complete mess kits ❷ into action, only a canteen cup ❸ and spoon (unwashed mess kits led to diarrhoea). In rear areas ❹, where kitchens and messes were established, hot meals were served ❺. However, these were still prepared from canned and dehydrated meats and vegetables. Fresh foods, such as eggs, milk, butter or meat, were unavailable on Guadalcanal because all shipping space was taken up by ammunition, fuel and other essential equipment.

Counting captured yen on Guadalcanal

The American campaign on Guadalcanal resulted in large amounts of Japanese money being captured on the island. Here, Marines count some of the captured currency in December 1942. The money on the table ❶ – 100,000 yen – was calculated as being worth $20,000 at pre-war conversion rates. In the background can be seen a Willys Jeep ❷ and a light sedan car ❸, the latter able to carry up to five passengers. The man on the far left wears the insignia of the Quartermaster's Department on his collar (the department responsible for all supply, the preparation of budget estimates, and the disbursement of all funds except pay of troops) ❹. This consisted of a gilt badge with a blue wheel. Two men are wearing what appear to be "cargo nets" over their M1 helmets ❺. These nets were made from vehicle nets cut down to size. No drawstring for tightening meant they had to be tucked in between the helmet and liner.

US Marine aircraft on Henderson Field

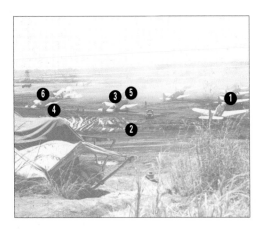

Marine Douglas SBD Dauntless dive-bombers ❶ warm up on Henderson Field ❷ on Guadalcanal in December 1942. The Dauntless was the standard shipborne dive-bomber of the US Navy from mid-1940 until November 1943. The Dauntless also saw intensive use with the Marines, flying from island bases. Marine Aircraft Group (MAG) 23 was the initial air unit participating on Guadalcanal, tasked with supporting the ground operations of the 1st Marine Division as well as the air defence of the island. MAG-23 included VMF-223 and -224 (fighter squadrons), and VMSB-231 and -232 (attack squadrons). The latter flew the Douglas SBD-3 Dauntless dive-bomber. The two-seat ❸ Dauntless carried bombs under the wings and the fuselage ❹ and had two fixed .5in Browning machine guns in the nose ❺. In addition, the aircraft was armed with twin .3in machine guns on a mounting in the rear of the turret ❻ for defence.

The 2d Marine Division on Guadalcanal

A Marine patrol of the 2d Marine Division ❶ pauses for a brief rest in a captured Japanese communications command post ❷ deep in the jungle beyond the Kokumbona River on Guadalcanal, 8 February 1943. These Marines are part of XIV Corps, which comprised the Americal Division, 25th Infantry Division, 43rd Infantry Division and 2d Marine Division. Organized Japanese resistance on the island ceased on 9 February. When the troops of the division boarded ship to leave Guadalcanal, some of them were so weakened by malaria they had to be carried on board. Observers remarked that they were young men grown old "with their skins cracked and furrowed and wrinkled" ❸. Some Marine units were still armed with Springfield rifles ❹. The Browning Automatic Rifle ❺ was the Marine squad automatic weapon. Note the BAR belt ❻, which had six pockets, each holding two 20-round BAR clips (a total of 12 clips).

Fully blooded Marine Corps Wildcat

A Marine Corps Grumman single-seat F4F Wildcat of fighter squadron VMF-223 ❶ on Henderson Field ❷ in early February 1943. Markings under the cockpit ❸ indicate that this plane has been credited with shooting down 19 Japanese aircraft, having been flown by several different pilots. The Wildcat was the primary US Navy and Marine Corps fighter during the first 18 months of World War II and was instrumental in establishing American air superiority over Guadalcanal, being part of the so-called "Cactus Air Force". The Japanese lost 650 aircraft between August and November 1942, and the F4Fs were responsible for most of these losses – their six wing-mounted .5in Browning machine guns ❹ could rip apart a Japanese Zero fighter in seconds. Though effective in the air, the Wildcat was tricky to fly and its landing gear ❺ was not well suited to the alternately muddy and dusty conditions of Henderson Field.

Paying respects to the fallen on New Georgia

In August 1943, at Enogai, on the northern side of New Georgia, an island in the Solomons, under the Stars and Stripes ❶, a Marine Corps chaplain ❷ holds a service beside the graves ❸ of those who fell in the battle against the Japanese a month earlier. These men ❹ are from Lieutenant-Colonel Griffith's 1st Raider Battalion, 1st Marine Raider Regiment, which attacked Enogai village on 10 July, losing 47 Marines killed, 74 wounded and 4 missing. The Japanese, though, suffered 350 dead; and the Marines captured 23 machine guns and four 140mm coastal defence guns. The operation had been particularly hard because the jungle terrain ❺ had made it impossible for the troops to carry all the food and ammunition they needed. They had fought for 30 hours without rations or water resupply. The destruction of the coastal guns at Enogai allowed US destroyers and torpedo boats to operate unhampered in the Kula Gulf.

Marines pilots scramble on Guadalcanal

Pilots of squadron VMF-124 ❶ race to their Chance Vought F4U1 Corsairs on Henderson Field, spring 1943. The Corsair's distinctive gull-wing design ❷ was the result of operational requirements. The powerful engine required a large-diameter propeller ❸ to absorb the power, but the landing gear ❹ had to be very strong to withstand the pounding of a carrier deck landing, and so a short, stout leg was needed. The gull-wing design allowed the huge prop to clear the deck while providing for a short landing gear. The wing also improved the aerodynamics of the intersection where the wing attaches to the fuselage, boosting the top speed. Armed with six wing-mounted .5in machine guns ❺, by the end of the Pacific War the Corsair had established an 11:1 kill ratio against enemy aircraft. VMF-124 was on Guadalcanal between 11 February and 7 September 1943. The F4U1 was called "Birdcage" due to its early type of canopy ❻.

A Mass before the beach assault

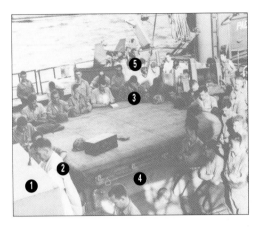

Off Tarawa Atoll, before a makeshift altar ❶, a chaplain ❷ conducts a Mass attended by Marines ❸ on board a troop transport ❹. A gun crew stands close to their 20mm Oerlikon ❺ in case of enemy attack. *TIME* correspondent Robert Sherrod was on board one such transport off Tarawa: "Ship life was dull. The men of the vessel and Marine Division fairly wilted in their crowded, hot quarters. They spent an hour each day cleaning rifles, sharpening bayonets, then another hour studying aerial photographs and contour maps of Betio, the little bird-shaped island that was the main fortification of Tarawa atoll. There was nothing else to do except see movies, read dog-eared magazines, play cards and sleep, which Marines can do at any time in any position on almost any given surface. The Marines seemed anything but excited. They had the calm confidence of a corps which assumes that it is the best fighting force in the world."

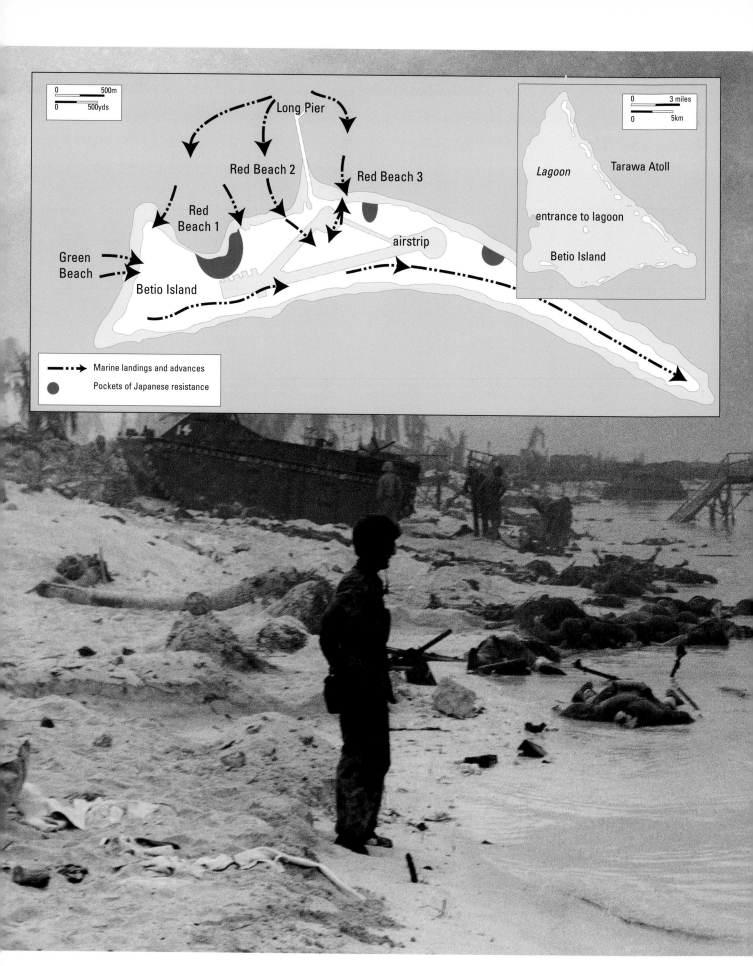

Long Pier

Red Beach 2

Red Beach 3

Red
Beach 1

Green
Beach

Betio Island

airstrip

0   500m
0   500yds

Marine landings and advances

Pockets of Japanese resistance

Lagoon

Tarawa Atoll

entrance to lagoon

Betio Island

0   3 miles
0   5km

Carnage on Red Beach 1, Betio Island

The scene on Red Beach 1 ❶, 22 November 1943. A Marine ❷ gazes at a Sherman tank ❸ that has struck a bomb or shell crater ❹ and lies disabled. To give the 2d Marine Division extra firepower, a company of M4A2 Shermans was attached to the invasion force: C Company, 1st Marine Corps Tank Battalion. Fourteen Shermans from C Company started out in landing craft: eight were to land on Red Beach 3, six on Red Beach 1. Only four of the latter made it onto the island. The M4s that made it on to land were knocked out as they drove parallel to the water to avoid running over the bodies of Marines killed in the initial assault wave ❺. On the left stands an LVT(1) amtrac ❻, which was part of Wave One of the Betio assault force. The LVTs approached the island in three waves: 42 LVT(1)s in Wave One, 24 LVT(2)s in Wave Two and 21 LVT(2)s in Wave Three. Marines fired 10,000 machine-gun rounds from their LVT(1)s in Wave One.

Carnage on Red Beach 2, Betio Island

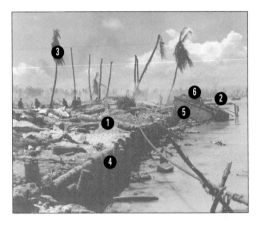

Combat Team 2 was the assault force at Tarawa, landing on Betio at 08:45 hours on 20 November in amtracs. This is the scene on Red Beach 2❶, on which the 2d Battalion, 2d Marines, landed (the inlet of Red Beach 1 ❷ is in the background) after the fighting had ended. Betio was devoid of natural defilade positions and favoured the defence. The island is less than 4.8km (3 miles) long, 730m (2400ft) across, covered in palm trees ❸ and contains no natural eleva-tion higher than 3m (10ft) above sea level. Japanese defences on the island included concrete and steel tetrahedrons, minefields and long strings of double-apron barbed wire protecting beach approaches. The Japanese also built a coconut log seawall ❹. Inland, tank traps protected fortified command bunkers and firing positions, and there were 500 pillboxes. This LVT(1)❺ was disabled on the seawall. It has two M1919 machine guns on skate mounts around the cargo area ❻.

Marine artillery comes ashore on Red Beach 2

The aftermath on Red Beach 2, Betio, November 1943. Men of the 2d Marines ❶ and their equipment litter the beach and illustrate just how quickly a beachhead could become cluttered after the initial landings (Red Beach 1 ❷ lies in the distance). As well as the ubiquitous machine-gun-armed LVT(1)s and LVT(2)s ❸, on the right stands a 105mm M2A1 howitzer ❹, two battalions of which equipped each Marine artillery regiment in 1943 (the other three battalions were equipped with 75mm howitzers). The gun was developed during the 1920s, finalized in the 1930s and went into production in 1941. It had a split trail, hydro-pneumatic recoil system, horizontal sliding breech and fired semi-fixed ammunition, carried in containers ❺. Ammunition types included high explosive, anti-tank, smoke and gas. It had a maximum range of 11km (6.8 miles). An experienced crew could fire up to 100 rounds per hour.

Fighting for the pier on Red Beach 3

Troops of the 2d Battalion, 8th Marines ❶, part of the 2d Marine Division, on Red Beach 3, Betio Island. They are fighting their way towards the Burns Philip Pier ❷, which was 366m (1200ft) east of the Long Pier, some with bayonets fixed ❸, some not. This unit suffered only 25 casualties when it landed on 20 November, and was reinforced by the 3rd Battalion, 8th Marines. This image encapsulates many of the problems faced by the Marines when clearing small Pacific islands. During the initial assault large numbers of amtracs could be lost to enemy fire ❹, mechanical breakdown or accidents (surviving vehicles were expected to return immediately to the transports to pick up more troops or ammunition). Thereafter the amtracs were expected to haul ammunition and supplies inland. The narrow beaches forced the men to bunch up around any cover ❺, making them vulnerable to enemy fire, especially mortar shells.

Wading ashore on "Bloody Tarawa"

Men of the 2d Marine Division ❶ wade towards Betio Island on 20 November 1943. These troops are not part of the first wave, which made the assault in amtracs. These men were transported by landing craft. However, due to the changing tides and depth of the water at the coral reef ❷ the transports had to unload their troops 450–900m (1476–2953ft) from the shore (many Marines were hit in the water by Japanese small-arms fire). By this time the 2d Marine Division was equipped with the two-piece camouflage utilities ❸. Though reversible, it was hardly ever worn brown-side out. The "green side" was always on display – dark and light greens and light and dark browns on a pale green background. The old M1923 cartridge belts ❹ were still being used, though at Tarawa the men were armed with M1 semi-automatic rifles ❺. The M1 helmets are covered by early helmet covers ❻. Note the M1 Carbine on the left ❼.

Marine Corps automatic firepower

A Marine machine gunner ❶ on Red Beach 3. Each rifle company in a Marine infantry regiment had a weapons platoon comprising a headquarters, a 19-man machine-gun section of three squads (one .3in M1919A4 machine gun ❷ in each squad) and a 16-man mortar section. The M1919A4 worked by using the recoil power of the barrel which, in a rearward thrust, unlocked the breech and sent it to the rear, extracting the spent case. Compression on the return spring then was used to strip a new round from the belt and chamber it. Fed by 150-round cloth belts, the gun could keep up a continuous rate of fire of around 60 rounds per minute for at least 30 minutes without overheating. Operated by a two-man crew, one Marine carried the gun and fired it; the other carried ammunition and sometimes a tripod, and was responsible for feeding the ammunition belts into the gun ❸. Note the ammunition box ❹ and the other two Marines with carbines ❺.

Air support for the Marines on the ground

Marines of the 2d Division ❶ duck for cover on Betio as a Grumman F6F Hellcat attacks ❷ enemy positions. Tarawa was a learning process as far as air support was concerned. Although it did little to win the battle, it proved that aircraft in direct support of troops on the ground was at least feasible. The plan had called for naval gunfire to hit the island until 30 minutes before the first wave was to land. Then the carrier air support was to take over until the LVTs ❸ were yards from the beach. The aircraft arrived at sunrise and attacked targets in the centre of the island. Their efforts were minimal, although the returning pilots claimed that nothing could be left alive on the island after the naval bombardment and air strikes were finished. The Marines had also requested that aircraft drop 2000lb "daisy-cutters" along the landing beaches ❹, and inland, to kill enemy troops and to level buildings, to no avail. A US tank is in the distance ❺.

A brief rest while Betio burns

Marines ❶, one armed with a Garand ❷, take a breather while one of their party relays messages and receives instructions by field telephone ❸. Black smoke from a burning enemy fuel dump ❹ darkens the sky in the background. The Marines suffered major communications problems at Tarawa. Their TBX and TBY radios, which were used for beach-to-beach communications, were bulky and hard to handle and were neither waterproof nor shockproof. Every radio set sent ashore became wet, rendering it unusable until it dried out. This interfered with effective naval gunfire and air support and made command and control by senior commanders all but impossible. The SCR-300 "walkie-talkie" and smaller SCR-536 "handy-talkie" entered Marine service in mid-1944. Because they still widely used field telephones, the Marines established the 1st–6th Separate Wire Platoons to lay and repair wires ❺.

Logistical problems on Betio Island

In a desperate effort to protect their ammunition and other supplies from Japanese air attack, Marines ❶ on the littered beach on Betio ❷ have covered their gear with camouflaged shelter-halfs ❸. During the first 24 hours of the battle the Marines had run dangerously low on rations, water, medical supplies and ammunition. Many supplies coming from ships offshore were simply dumped ❹ on the beach (Admiral Hill, the amphibious task force commander, wanted the transports unloaded as quickly as possible to protect his vessels from enemy air and naval attack). The Marines were thus forced to strip the dead of their ammunition, canteens and first aid kits. Fortunately, Japanese air attacks never materialized. In the water can be seen an LVT(2) Water Buffalo amtrac ❺, which was first used at Tarawa and thereafter became the main Marine Corps amtrac until mid-1944. It was capable of carrying up to 24 troops.

Keeping up the pressure on the defenders

Two Marines ❶ carrying machine-gun ammunition ❷ race forward during the fighting on Betio. In total, 5000 Marines had stormed the beaches of Betio on 20 November; 1500 were dead, wounded or missing by nightfall. The survivors held less than a quarter of a square mile of sand and coral. The commander of the 2d Marines, Colonel David M. Shoup, later described the location of his beachhead lines on the night of the 20th as "a stock market graph". His men took up the best fighting positions they could find, either in shellholes inland ❸ or along the seawall. These Marines are attempting to clear a Japanese bunker on the right ❹. Despite the six million pounds of American naval explosives that were hurled against the island before the Marines landed, many of the shells bounced off the ground ❺ and into the ocean beyond due to a flat trajectory, and thus many of the Japanese strongpoints were unscathed.

Medal of Honor winner on Tarawa

This image shows the assault by 1st Lieutenant Alexander Bonnyman ❶, Executive Officer of the 2d Battalion Shore Party, 18th Marines, 2d Marine Division, on Betio on 22 November 1943. His Medal of Honor citation stated: "fearlessly exposing himself to the merciless slash of hostile fire as he stormed the formidable bastion ❷, [Bonnyman] directed the placement of demolition charges in both entrances and seized the top of the bombproof position ❸, flushing more than 100 of the enemy who were instantly cut down, and effecting the annihilation of approximately 150 troops inside the emplacement. Assailed by additional Japanese after he had gained his objective, he made a heroic stand on the edge of the structure ❹, defending his strategic position with indomitable determination in the face of the desperate charge, and killing three of the enemy before he fell, mortally wounded." Note the Marine with the flamethrower ❺.

Hell on a former tropical paradise

Among the dead **1**, the bullet-shredded palm trees **2** and the shell-blasted **3** ruins on Tarawa, a soldier of the 2d Marine Division **4** goes through the wreckage of a building in search of wounded. Unfortunately for the Marines on Tarawa, the high-explosive shells used by bombardment ships lying offshore usually detonated before they penetrated Japanese bunkers. This produced an impressive explosion and a lot of smoke **5** but did little actual damage. Marines were thus forced to fight singly, or in ones and twos, against the defenders. The Japanese boasted that it would take a million men 10 years to take Tarawa – it took the Marines 76 hours. Admiral Chester Nimitz later wrote of the battle on Tarawa: "But at the time we did the best with what we had, and in that 'best' was the resolute courage of our Marines, who in spite of all obstacles seized the island." Marine casualties were 837 killed and 2296 wounded.

Casualty evacuation at Tarawa

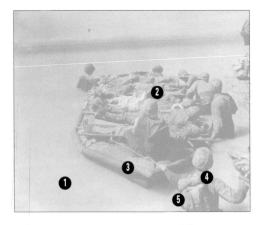

At Tarawa some 2300 Americans were wounded. Because of the coral reefs and shallow waters ❶ hospital ships were unable to get close to shore to receive casualties. Therefore, the wounded had to be floated out to the ships, as here ❷. Beyond the reef line they were loaded on to landing craft, then taken to troop transports operating as hospitals. A US medical report later stated: "The average wounding rate of 11.04 men per 1,000 men per day was seven times the average rate for a division in combat and more than twice the average for virtually all other types of action. Casualty rates as high as 25% of landing force personnel have occurred in such heavily opposed amphibious actions as the 76-hour invasion of Tarawa." The vessel here is a 10-man landing craft, rubber (large), or LCR(L) ❸. It could be fitted with an Evinrude outboard motor for a speed of 4.5 knots. Note the camouflaged poncho ❹ and entrenching tool ❺.

The few who chose surrender over death

Troops from the 2d Marine Division guard Japanese prisoners **1** on Betio while a medic **2** treats one of their badly wounded comrades **3**. Of the 2800 members of the Japanese Special Naval Landing Force that defended Betio, only 17 survived to surrender. And only 129 of the 2000 Korean construction troops on the island survived. This pattern was repeated elsewhere on Tarawa Atoll. For example, during the battle at Buariki on 26 November the entire Japanese garrison of 156 fought to the death (the Marines losing 34 killed and 56 wounded). By 1943, each 12-man Marine rifle squad comprised a squad leader (sergeant), assistant squad leader (corporal), two automatic riflemen, two assistants and six riflemen – a weapons mix of 10 M1 Garands **4** and 2 M1918A2 BARs. The M1 Carbine **5** was issued to officers, weapons crewmen, radio operators, drivers and headquarters personnel as a personal defence weapon.

The dogs of war on Bougainville

Dogs and their handlers of the Marine Corps' 1st War Dog Platoon on Bougainville, November 1943 ❶. The platoon, commanded by Lieutenant Clyde A. Henderson, served with the 2d Raider Battalion on Bougainville (the Marines landed on the island on 1 November, the 24 canine members of the platoon going ashore just one hour after the first Marines hit the beach). The platoon consisted of 48 enlisted men working in pairs as handlers ❷ for the 21 Dobermans ❸ and three German Shepherds ❹, plus six enlisted instructors and headquarters personnel. The dogs' keen eyesight and sense of smell was a great advantage in jungle terrain ❺. As well as carrying messages, the dogs led infantry points on advances, explored caves, pillboxes and dugouts, and scouted fortified positions. The dogs and their handlers were credited with leading 350 patrols in the final phase of the campaign.

The 1st Marine Division on New Britain

Troops of the 17,850-strong 1st Marine Division ❶ pour ashore from LST (Landing Ship, Tank) vessels ❷ at Cape Gloucester, New Britain, in December 1943. The main objective was the capture and expansion of the Japanese airfield at Cape Gloucester, to contribute to the isolation of the major Japanese base at Rabaul, part of Operation Cartwheel, the Allied strategic plan in the Southwest Pacific area and Pacific Ocean areas in 1943–44. Powered by two General Motors 12-567 diesel engines, each LST had a top speed of 12 knots. Each ship had a crew of 8–10 officers and 100–115 enlisted men ❸ and could carry up to 140 troops ❹. Armament ❺ varied, but could include five 40mm anti-aircraft gun mounts, six 20mm anti-aircraft gun mounts, two .5in machine guns and four .3in machine guns. The landings, codenamed Dovetail, took place on 26 December, and by the end of the day 11,000 Marines had been landed.

Marine Raiders in the Solomon Islands

Marine Raiders ❶ gather in front of a captured Japanese dugout ❷ on Cape Totkina, Bougainville, Solomon Islands, in January 1944. Bougainville is 48km (30 miles) wide and 200km (125 miles) long, and the 2d and 3rd Raider Battalions, commanded by Lieutenant-Colonels Joseph S. McCaffery and Fred S. Beans, suffered heavy casualties during their two-month campaign. These two battalions were grouped under the 2d Raider Regiment (Provisional). The Raiders were among the first Marine units to receive the two-piece camouflage utilities ❸ and helmet covers ❹. Weapons included M1 rifles ❺ and carbines, M1928 BARs, M1879 and M1912 shotguns, M1928, M1A1 and M55 sub-machine guns and M1911A1 handguns. One Raider is holding a Japanese Arisaka rifle ❻. By February the Raiders had been disbanded (as the Marines were considered to be élite soldiers, having an élite unit within the Corps was considered unnecessary).

Survivors of a banzai charge on Tinian

Al Perry fought in A Company ❶, 1st Battalion, 24th Marines, 4th Marine Division, on Tinian. "This picture was taken on August 25, 1944 after we finished fighting on Tinian. We had lost 102 men on Saipan. We hit Tinian with 155 men. Twelve hours later we had only 62 men left. These are the remains of our company after we had secured Tinian. Many of these men were wounded ❷ during the hand-to-hand battle we had with the Japs the first night, I will never forget this battle; we had suffered horrible casualties. Most of us were covered with small pieces of human body parts after it was over." Tinian's flat, rolling terrain ❸ allowed the Marines to make a rapid advance against fanatical Japanese resistance. The captured Japanese battle flags ❹ have messages of support and best wishes written on them ❺. Tinian was declared secure on 1 August 1944, by which time the Marines had suffered 2300 casualties.

Clearing the Marshalls, atoll by atoll

Marines ❶ on Namur, Kwajalein Atoll, on 2 February 1944. They are taking advantage of a trench ❷ dug and vacated by the Japanese until they receive the order to advance. The smoke ❸ is a result of the bombardment that preceded the Marine invasion, while the trees ❹ bear witness to heavy small-arms fire. The sand ❺ islands of Roi and Namur are only a few feet above sea level. Roi had been cleared to make way for a Japanese airstrip, while Namur was crowded with palms and enemy held buildings. The garrison comprised 3563 men of the 61st Guard Force Dispatched Force, 24th Air Flotilla HQ, aircraft service personnel and labourers. The two lead battalions of the 23rd Marines landed on Roi, and the two lead battalions of the 24th Marines assaulted Namur. Both islands were secure by 2 February, the 4th Marine Division suffering 313 killed and 502 wounded. Only 91 Japanese surrendered; the rest were killed.

Storming the beach on Saipan

Marines take cover behind a sand dune ❶ on Saipan. Behind them is an LVT(2) Water Buffalo ❷, the main Marine amtrac from November 1943 until mid-1944. In the background can be seen an LVT(A) 4 amphibious tank, which entered production in early 1944 ❸. Its open-topped turret housed the short-barrelled 75mm M3 gun ❹. Secondary armament comprised a .5in machine gun mounted on top of the turret ❺. First used on Saipan, the Marines eventually took delivery of a total of 533 LVT(A) 4s (the US Army took delivery of a further 1307). Amphibious tanks provided direct fire support for Marines until the medium tanks could be brought ashore. They performed well enough in the beach area, but when they moved inland their high profile presented an excellent target for Japanese anti-tank guns. In addition, they were slow – 32kmh (20mph) – and had poor cross-country mobility due to their low ground clearance.

Hit by an enemy sniper on Saipan

A Marine ❶ has just been hit by a Japanese sniper on the island of Saipan, which in 1944 was covered in suger-cane, scrub trees ❷, brush and high grass. The Japanese had built airfields on both ends of the island, the second largest in the Marianas chain. The 2d and 4th Marine Divisions landed on 15 June, the island having been bombarded by the navy for two days, and by aircraft for more than a month (napalm was first used on Saipan). Most Marines battalions came ashore on beaches that were at least 549m (1800ft) wide, supported by rocket ships as they did so. The equipment carried by these Marines is typical of this stage of the war, and reflects lessons learnt in earlier campaigns, such as carrying two canteens instead of one ❸. The entrenching tools ❹ are the M1910 model, with M1923 cartridge belts ❺. All the men are armed with M1 Carbines ❻, indicating they could be service personnel.

Fighting on the outskirts of Garapan

On the outskirts of Garapan ❶, the administrative centre on Saipan on the west coast of the island, two members of the 2d Marine Division ❷ search for the enemy. The location shows signs of having been heavily shelled ❸. The Marine on the left is armed with the 2.36in M1A1 rocket launcher, or bazooka ❹. First used as an anti-tank weapon, its numbers within a Marine division were almost doubled in mid-1943 when it was discovered to be very effective against enemy bunkers. In 1944 the M1A1 began to be replaced by the 2.36in M9A1 and M18 rocket launchers, which had greater range due to a lengthened tube that could be broken down into two sections for ease of carrying. The M18 was developed specifically for the Pacific theatre, having an aluminium tube to prevent rusting. Though much of Saipan is flat ❺, making movement on foot easy, there are areas of swamp that are restrictive for both people and vehicles.

Marine tank-infantry teams on Guam

The island of Guam was invaded on 21 July 1944. Beforehand special emphasis had been placed on tank-infantry team training, which bore dividends during the campaign. Here, infantry from the 21st Marines ❶ work in conjunction with M4A2 Sherman tanks ❷ of the 3rd Tank Battalion as they drive inland from the beach. Marine tanks went into action "buttoned up" ❸ because the main threat was from Japanese infantry, not tanks, and they also removed turret-mounted machine guns ❹ to stop enemy soldiers jumping on the tanks and using them against Marines. Accompanying Marines had the job of not only alerting tankers of enemy infantry attacks but also of the presence of anti-tank guns and other dangers they could not see. This procedure was called "physical protection" (Marines were able to talk to the crew via telephone or by hand and arm signals). Drums ❺ of diesel fuel indicate that this is a posed photograph.

Marine rocket detachment in action

The 1st Rocket Detachment (Provisional) ❶ in action on the island of Saipan ❷ in July 1944, part of the 4th Marine Division's Support Group. The Marines' first attempt at a rocket unit was the 1st Corps Experimental Rocket Platoon in June 1943, which was armed with 4.5in T27E1 single-tube rocket launchers and 2.36in M1 bazookas. In 1944 the 1st, 2d, 3rd, 4th and 5th Rocket Detachments (Provisional) were formed, each one being assigned to a Marine division. Each detachment had three officers and 53 enlisted men organized into a small headquarters and two sections (nicknamed "Buck Rogers Men" after the science fiction comic book hero). Each section had six one-ton International M-3 trucks ❸ mounting three launcher racks ❹ containing 4.5in M8 rockets ❺. Each rocket had a range of 4.2km (2.6 miles). The detachments provided an area fire capability for counterbattery missions. Saipan was their first time in action.

Marine skirmish line advancing on Tinian

The island of Tinian is 16.4km (10.25 miles) long and 8km (5 miles) wide, with Mount Lasso dominating its northern end. When the Marines invaded in 1944 sugarcane covered 80 percent of the island. Here, a platoon from the 2d Marines ❶ has formed a skirmish line while a Stinson L-5 Sentinel observation plane ❷ flies overhead. The 2d Marines, part of Combat Team 2 (2d Marine Division), had landed on Tinian at noon on 25 July. In open terrain, such as here, Marine infantry working with tanks operated a tactic known as "support by fire", in which a squad of riflemen watched over each tank and shot down any enemy infantry that showed themselves. As well as small arms ❸, grenades were essential tools for clearing enemy positions, and one Marine has a fragmentation grenade attached to his webbing ❹. The high ground ❺ in the distance is part of a long spine extending almost due south from Mount Lasso.

A Marine "peashooter" opens fire

On the island of Tinian ❶, a 75mm M1A1 howitzer blasts ❷ a cave full of Japanese from the brink of a sheer cliff. The gun has been lashed securely ❸ in its position after parts were carried by hand to the cliff's edge ❹. The M1A1 was first used in combat in 1942 in the Philippines. Though by 1944 the Marines were contemplating moving solely to the 105mm M2A1 howitzer, the 75mm was still popular in the Corps because it could be transported in all landing craft and amtracs; could be manhandled into firing positions, as here; and could be broken down into six loads for transport, either by mules or men, over rough terrain for direct fire against caves and pillboxes (it weighed 587.9kg – 1296lb – with a barrel length of 1.194m – 3.9ft). It could be re-assembled in three minutes. It was also reliable. When set up, a crew ❺ could fire up to six rounds per minute. By 1944, a Marine artillery regiment had two 75mm artillery battalions.

A coral and sand wasteland called Peleliu

Marines with M1 submachine guns **1** give covering fire to advancing 1st Marine Division troops on Peleliu. The latter, part of the Palau Islands, was invaded in September 1944. The ground **2** in this image – coral boulders and sand – is typical of the terrain encountered by the Marines during the battle for the island. Equipment on display includes an M1910 Pick-mattock **3**, canteen **4** and five-cell, 20-round magazine pockets **5**. The Thompson M1 and M1A1 submachine guns began to be issued to Marine units in 1943. They had a 30-round magazine but could also use the M1928A1's 20-round magazine. A problem with the Thompson was that it sounded like a Japanese 6.5mm light machine gun and so often drew friendly fire when used. In addition, its .45in round had poor penetration through dense brush and bamboo. Around 10,900 Japanese were killed on Peleliu; Marine casualties numbered 6526, of whom 1252 were killed.

Using the enemy's airfield on Peleliu

Looking down from the control tower, the tent area ❶ of the 2d Marine Air Wing (MAW) fringes the fighter taxiway ❷ on the north side of the airstrip on Peleliu, 17 October 1944 (2d MAW was originally commissioned in July 1941, its first home base being San Diego, with two squadrons there as well as four others in Hawaii). On 26 September, Marine Airbase (MAB) Peleliu had been declared operational, with 24 F4U fighter-bombers landing from the carrier USS *Lexington*. US aircraft had begun landing on the airfield on 18 September, and six days later the first Marine fighter units of Marine Air Group (MAG) 11 landed there. With ongoing ground operations close by, fighters from Marine Fighter Squadrons (VMF) 541, 114, 122 and 121 flew from Peleliu. There is a mix of Marine Corps aircraft on the airstrip, including a Consolidated Catalina ❸, Douglas Dakota ❹, Grumman Avenger ❺ and Lockheed Lightning ❻.

"Like all the cats in the world having kittens"

LVT(4) amtracs ❶ mounting machine guns ❷ approach the island of Iwo Jima on 19 February 1945, carrying troops of the 5th Marine Division ❸. The division's beaches were to the northeast of Mount Suribachi. For the landing on the island the four amphibious tractor battalions of the invasion force had a mixture of LVT(2)s and LVT(4)s. The LVT(4) was essentially a remodelled LVT(2), with the engine moved from the rear. This produced a larger cargo area and allowed a rear loading ramp to be installed. For additional protection, appliqué armour could be attached to the front ❹ and sides ❺, but this reduced payload. In the background can be seen *LST-70* ❻. The LSTs (tank landing ships) loaded amtracs and DUKWs into the water, in a scene described as "like all the cats in the world having kittens". Operation Detachment, the capture of Iwo Jima, involved the 3rd, 4th and 5th Marine Divisions – a total of 65,953 men.

D-Day at Iwo Jima, 19 February 1945

With the island wreathed in smoke as Iwo Jima is pummelled by naval gun-fire ❶, Marines of the 4th and 5th Divisions approach beaches Green, Red, Yellow and Blue abreast, initially encountering little enemy resistance. The first five assault waves ❷ were made up of only LVTs, with the first wave consisting of 68 LVTs ❸. These small craft reached the beach at 09:00 hours under light gunfire and the next four waves followed within 23 minutes. Mount Suribachi, a Japanese strongpoint ❹, dominated the landing beaches, which were, from left to right, Green❺, Red 1❻, Red 2❼, Yellow 1, Yellow 2, Blue 1 and Blue 2. Unfortunately for the Marines, the Japanese defenders on Iwo Jima were dug into caves, fortifications and tunnels, and the preliminary air and naval strikes had left them largely unscathed. The Marines were about to go up against nearly 22,000 enemy troops defending the most heavily fortified place on earth.

The 4th Marine Division hits Blue Beach

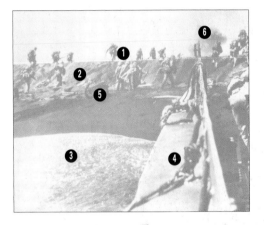

The 4th Marine Division ❶ lands on Iwo Jima, 19 February 1945. Planners believed that the beaches would present few problems for the assault forces. The beach resembled a gravel dump with brown volcanic ash and black cinders. When the men got ashore they found that it was difficult to crawl up the loose sand banks – these volcanic ash terraces ❷ rose 4.5m (15ft) in some places. In addition, these terraces hampered the progress of the LVTs, because the cinders and ash offered poor traction. Finally, the surf ❸ broke directly on the beach, carrying the smaller craft sideways. And when wreckage began collecting in the landing areas, later waves of landing craft were blocked. These men are coming ashore from a Higgins Boat ❹, which indicates they are not in the initial assault waves. They are pulling heavy machine guns mounted on carriages ❺. The explosions ❻ suggest that the fighting has moved inland.

In the ruins of Motoyama on Iwo Jima

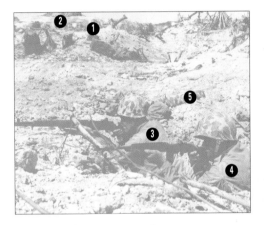

Two troops from the 3rd Marine Division, probably the 21st Marines, in hastily prepared positions amid the ruins of Motoyama village on Iwo Jima. The sulphur mine ❶ and refinery ❷ are in the background. Private Robert K. Marshall ❸ is armed with a Garand, while Corporal Allan L. Griffin ❹ shoulders an M1 Carbine. Both men are wearing herringbone twill combat fatigues and camouflaged helmet covers. Note the camouflage poncho ❺. The 21st Marines, supported by an intense naval and artillery barrage, had entered and cleared the ruins of Motoyama village on the last day of February, and the 3rd Battalion of the regiment had continued the advance and taken up position on some high ground overlooking the unfinished Airfield No 3. As it was doing so, the 1st and 2d Battalions had to contend with a mass of uncleared enemy positions and were soon fighting at close quarters using demolitions and flamethrowers.

The Marines take Mount Suribachi

It was the job of the 28th Regiment, 5th Division, to capture Mount Suribachi ❶ on Iwo Jima. On the morning of 23 February, a patrol ❷ of 40 men from the 3rd Platoon, E Company, 2d Battalion, 28th Marines, led by 1st Lieutenant Harold G. Schrier, stormed up the mountain's slopes. Of 40 Marines, 36 were killed or wounded in later fighting on Iwo Jima. Schrier was awarded the Navy Cross for the first flag raising, and on 24 March he led the defence during a desperate Japanese attack on Iwo Jima, earning him a Silver Star. The first Stars and Stripes flag ❸ raised on Mount Suribachi was obtained from attack transport USS *Missoula*, and hoisted on a 6m (20ft) section of Japanese pipe ❹ at 10:20 hours. Several hours later, a 2.4m- (8ft-) long battle ensign, obtained from tank landing ship *LST-779*, was raised, resulting in Associated Press photographer Joe Rosenthal's famous image of the flag raising on Mount Suribachi.

The men behind the Marine Corps legend

Joe Rosenthal's iconic image of the flag raising on Mount Suribachi, 23 February 1945. The men are, from left to right: Ira Hayes (1923–55) ❶: a Native American who survived Iwo Jima but suffered from post-traumatic stress which led to him becoming an alcoholic. Of Ira's platoon of 45 men, only 5 survived the fighting on Iwo Jima. Franklin Sousley (1925–45) ❷: the winner of the Purple Heart, he was the last flag raiser to die on Iwo Jima, being killed on 21 March. Czech-born Michael Strank (1919–45) ❸ was killed by friendly fire on 1 March. Rene Gagnon (1925–79) ❹ carried the flag up Mount Suribachi. He survived the campaign and served until April 1946. John Bradly (1923–94) ❺, winner of the Purple Heart and Navy Cross, was a Navy Corpsman who "just jumped in to lend a hand" on Suribachi. Harlon Block (1924–45) ❻, second-in-command to Strank, was killed in a mortar attack just a few hours after him.

The slow, costly advance on Iwo Jima

Marine riflemen ❶ fire on Japanese positions from behind a burning M4 Sherman ❷ during the assault on the town of Nishi, Iwo Jima, in March 1945. The 3rd, 4th and 5th Marine Tank Battalions fought on the island, at one point on the Motoyama Plateau combining for a 100-tank attack. On the island M4s had 102mm (4in) layers of reinforced concrete, supported by wooden planks, attached to their sides ❸ as protection against Japanese 47mm anti-tank rounds. Note the canvas field leggings ❹ worn by the Marine on the left. In early March the 5th Marine Division continued its offensive along the northwest coast of the island, with the 26th Marines attacking Hill 362B and the 28th Marines attacking Nishi Ridge. Both regiments suffered heavily (particularly the 26th) when they came under intense artillery and machine-gun fire, but the 26th reached the summit of Hill 362B and the 28th Marines took Nishi Ridge ❺.

Marine Corps logistics on Iwo Jima

To keep them at their peak operational capacity, the Marine divisions on Iwo Jima required a continuous flow of food, water, fuel and ammunition, which meant a continuous stream of supplies being landed on the invasion beaches. Here, Marines unload supplies ❶ from *LSM-201* ❷, *LST-807* ❸, *LSM-391* ❹ and other amphibious warships. Each Landing Ship Medium (LSM) was capable of transporting up to 168 tonnes (165 tons) of supplies, or five medium or three heavy tanks, or six LVTs, or nine DUKWs. Defensive armament included one single bow-mounted 40mm anti-aircraft gun position ❺ and four single 20mm anti-aircraft gun mounts. Landing the ships was a tricky business. The log of *LST-807* reported: "Let go stern anchor, hit beach at 2/3 speed and piled up on top of wrecked vehicles, of which the beach was covered. After hitting the beach, we could just make out a pin point of light which was the beach marker."

Insatiable ammunition requirements

A Marine 105mm M2A1 howitzer **①** opens fire on Iwo Jima. An experienced crew could fire up to 100 rounds per hour, which entailed considerable ammunition expenditure. Indeed, on several days Marine artillery battalions fired more ammunition **②** than was unloaded during the same period. The 168 howitzers of the 14 battalions on Iwo Jima fired a total of 450,156 rounds, broken down thus: 48 75mm howitzers (181,510); 96 105mm howitzers (224,851); and 24 155mm howitzers (43,795). On Iwo Marine divisional artillery regiments had two battalions with M2A1 howitzers and two of 75mm howitzers, though in 1944 the decision had been taken to equip regiments solely with the 105mm to take advantage of its longer range and more lethal effects. Most of the crew are wearing camouflage ponchos **③** as protection against the rain. On the left a Marine is receiving orders by field telephone **④** (note the KA-Bar knife attached to his belt) **⑤**.

Fire and movement on Okinawa

Marines of the 2d Battalion, 1st Marines, fighting on Wana Ridge, Okinawa, May 1945. On the left Davis Hargraves ❶ provides covering fire with his M1 Thompson submachine gun ❷ while BAR man Gabriel Chavarria ❸ moves forward (he is wearing an M1937 BAR magazine belt) ❹. On 14 May the 1st Marine Division had entered the Wana Draw, formed from the reverse slope of Wana Ridge on its left and the forward slope of another ridge to its right. The ridge ❺, a long coral spine running out of northern Shuri, was lined on both sides with fortified tombs. Marine bazooka rounds, rifle grenades, white phosphorus and fragmentation grenades were hurled against the caves on the reverse slope of Wana. But replying Japanese mortar and sniper fire was still heavy, forcing Marines to take cover among the tombs and coral. On 22 May, Japanese troops tried to drive the 1st Marines off Wana Ridge but failed.

The 6th Marine Division in Naha, Okinawa

Temporarily pinned down by enemy fire, these men of the 6th Marine Division take cover behind a wall during the battle among the wrecked buildings and rubble of Naha, the capital city of Okinawa, June 1945. As they wait, one Leatherneck peers cautiously around a corner ❶ to see what is ahead. The Marine in the centre is armed with an M1 Carbine ❷, attached to which is an M8 grenade launcher ❸. Unlike the M1 rifle, the carbine could fire semi automatic with the launcher mounted. The M8 clamped on the end of the barrel and was held in place by a wing nut. The carbine is also fitted with a canvas pouch on the stock, which carries two 15-round magazines ❹. Though the city itself had no tactical value, Japanese snipers in walled compounds ❺ around houses and enemy machine guns emplaced in burial tombs caused a number of Marine casualties. The city was heavily shelled and bombed in May 1945.

"Blowtorch and corkscrew" tactics

Okinawa was infested with fortified caves ❶ and dugouts. Japanese troops were relatively safe from air and artillery attack inside the caves, after which they emerged to attack American troops with mortars and grenades. To clear caves of Japanese defenders the Americans came up with a novel tactic called "blowtorch and corkscrew", a term coined by Commander of the Tenth Army, Major-General Simon Bolivar Buckner. Rather than venture into said caves, troops would seal the caves to entomb burned, screaming Japanese. Flamethrowing tanks provided the blowtorch, while dynamite charges and grenades were the corkscrews. If tanks were not available, explosive charges ❷ were hurled into the caves, while infantry waited outside to mow down any survivors who crawled out. The weapons mix of these Marines comprises M1 rifles ❸ and Thompson submachine guns❹. One Marine is wearing a utility cap❺.

Okinawa – a land of 1000 ridges

The island of Okinawa consists of rugged, high hills in the north and ridges and hills ❶ in the south, which are honeycombed with caves. In addition, the Japanese Thirty-Second Army that defended the island had built more than 96km (60 miles) of tunnels. The ridges, caves and tunnels all had to be cleared by Marines and GIs in a slow, bloody advance. Here, Marines ❷ on a ridge ❸ pour small arms fire into a Japanese position as enemy shells hit the ground nearby ❹. The M9 bazooka ❺ had a tube that could be broken down for ease of carrying. Bazookas were used to knock out reinforced enemy positions. The Japanese lost 110,000 killed and wounded, 7400 more were taken prisoner and more than 120,000 Okinawan civilians were killed. Total American battle casualties were 49,151, of which 12,520 were killed or missing and 36,631 wounded. Of these, the Marines lost 2938 killed and missing and 13,708 wounded.

US Marine Corps Cemetery, Iwo Jima

Prayer at the Marine Cemetery, Iwo Jima, 26 March 1945, by Lieutenant Roland Gittelsohn: *"This is perhaps the grimmest, and surely the holiest, task we have faced since D-Day. Here before us lie the bodies of comrades and friends. Men who until yesterday or last week laughed with us, joked with us, trained with us. Men who were on the same ships with us, and went over the sides with us as we prepared to hit the beaches of this island. Men who fought with us and feared with us. Under one of these Christian crosses, or beneath a Jewish Star of David, there may rest now a man who was destined to be a great prophet ... to find the way, perhaps, for all to live in plenty, with poverty and hardship for none. Now they lie here silently in this sacred soil, and we gather to consecrate this earth in their memory. It is not easy to do so. Some of us have buried our closest friends here. We saw these men killed before our very eyes."*

Index

1st Marine Division 11, 13, 75, 97, 119
1st Rocket Detachment 91
1st Tank Battalion, A Company 15
2d Marine Division 35, 49, 53, 57, 65, 67, 71, 87, 93
3rd Battalion, 4th Marine Regiment 7
3rd Marine Division 107
4th Battalion, 11th Marines 17
4th Marine Division 81, 105
4th Marine Regiment 7
5th Marine Division 11, 101
6th Marine Division 121
21st Marines 89
28th Marines 113

A
airfield, Cape Gloucester 75
artillery support 17, 49
automatic firepower 55

B
banzai charge 79
Bataan Death March 9
Beach Red assault, Guadalcanal 11
beach terraces 105
Betio Island 47–53, 57–63
"Birdcage" F4U1 41
"Blowtorch" tactic 123
Bonnyman, Lieutenant Alexander 65
Bougainville 73, 77
Bushido code 9

C
camouflage uniform 53, 61, 77, 107, 117
Camp O'Donnell 9
Cape Gloucester airfield 75
captured currency 31
casualty rates 69, 71, 125
cemetery, Iwo Jima Island 127
Chance Vought F4U1 Corsairs 41

commanders, Guadalcanal 25
communications 21, 59
"Corkscrew" tactic 123
Corps commanders 25
Corregidor 9

D
"Death March" 9
Diseases 23
    malaria 35
dive-bombers, Marine Douglas SBD Dauntless 33
dog handlers 73

F
F4F Wildcat 37
F4U fighter-bombers 99
field telephones 59

G
Garapan, Saipan 87
graves, New Georgia 38
Grumman F4F Wildcat 37
Grumman F6F Hellcat 57
Guadalcanal 13–37, 41
    see also Red Beach
Guam 89

H
HBM2 .5in machine gun 27
Henderson Field 15, 23, 25, 33, 37, 41
Henderson, Major Lofton 23

I
Iwo Jima island 101–7
    ammunition 117
    cemetery 127
    logistics 115
    Nishi 113

J
Japanese camp 13
Japanese forces 9, 11, 47, 125

K
Kwajalein Atoll, Namur 81

L
Lindberg 109
LVT(A)4 amphibious tank 83

M
M1 Garand semi-automatic rifle 13
M1 helmets 11, 31
M1A1 howitzer 95
M2A1 howitzer 49, 117
M2A4 light tank 15
M4A2 Sherman tank 45, 113
M5 gun 15
M8 grenade launcher 121
M9 bazooka 125
M1903 Springfield bolt-action rifles 19
M1910 Pick-mattock 97
M1917 machine guns 7
M1917A1 "dishpan" helmets 7
M1919A4 machine gun 15, 55
M1936 canvas field bag 11
M1941 haversack 11
Marine 155mm howitzers 17
Marine Aircraft Group (MAG) 33
Marine cemetery, Iwo Jima 127
Marine Corps aircraft 99
Marine Corps Browning HBM2 machine gun 27
Marine Corps Wildcat 37
Marine Douglas Dauntless dive-bombers 33
Marine raiders 77
Marine uniforms 7, 9, 19
    see also camouflage
Marshalls 81
meals, rations 29
medal, Purple Heart and Silver Star 109
Medal of Honor 65
message centre, Guadalcanal 21
money, captured currency 31
Motoyama village, Iwo Jima island 107

Mount Lasso, Tinian 93
Mount Suribachi 101, 103, 109, 111

N
Navajo code talkers 21
New Britain 75
New Georgia, service for dead 39
Nishi, Iwo Jima 113

O
Okinawa 119, 121, 123, 125

P
Peleliu
    airstrip 99
    Palau Islands 97
perimeter machine gun 27
prisoners 9

R
Red Beach 1 45
Red Beach 2 47, 49
Red Beach 3 51, 55
religious mass 43
rocket detachment 91

S
Saipan 83, 85, 91
Solomon Islands, Marine Raiders 77
Stars and Stripes flag 109, 111

T
tank-infantry team training 89
Tarawa Atoll 43, 53–9, 65–9
Tinian 79, 93, 95
transportation of supplies 115

V
VMF-124 squadron 41

W
War Dog Platoon 73
Water Buffalo LVT(2) 61, 83
Wildcat (F4F) fighter squadron 37